Google Drive & Docs In 30 Minutes

"I bought your Google Docs guide myself (my new company uses it) and it was really handy. I loved it."

"I have been impressed by the writing style and how easy it was to get very familiar and start leveraging Google Docs. I can't wait for more titles. Nice job!"

Twitter In 30 Minutes

"A perfect introduction to Twitter. Quick and easy read with lots of photos. I finally understand the # symbol!"

"Clarified any issues and concerns I had and listed some excellent precautions."

Excel Basics In 30 Minutes

"Fast and easy. The material presented is very basic but it is also accessible with step-by-step screenshots and a friendly tone more like a friend or co-worker explaining how to use Excel than a technical manual."

"An excellent little guide. For those who already know their way around Excel, it'll be a good refresher course. Definitely plan on passing it around the office."

LinkedIn In 30 Minutes

"This book does everything it claims. It gives you a great introduction to LinkedIn and gives you tips on how to make a good profile."

"I already had a LinkedIn account, which I use on a regular basis, but still found the book very helpful. The author gave examples and explained why it is important to detail and promote your account."

Dropbox In 30 Minutes

"I was intimidated by the whole idea of storing my files in the cloud, but this book took me through the process and made it so easy."

"This was truly a 30-minute tutorial and I have mastered the basics without bugging my 20-year-old son! Yahoo!"

"Very engaging and witty."

Genealogy
Basics

In 30 Minutes

**The quick guide to creating a
family tree, building connections
with relatives, and discovering the
stories of your ancestors**

Shannon Combs-Bennett

*To Donna,
Happy Researching!
Shannon Combs-Bennett*

To my husband and children: Thank you for putting up with my cemetery side trips and long stories about our ancestors. You are the reason I work.

To my father: Thank you for teaching me to love history, and that long road trips need not be boring when you can discover something new. You always have something new to teach me.

To my mother (1956-2016): Even though you were taken too soon from us, your spirit will shine on through our family, and through my stories. Thank you for showing me that being a strong, independent, and smart woman was perfectly okay.

Contents

Contents

Contents

Introduction

When I was a child, I liked to listen to my family share family stories. At six years of age, sometimes I would hide away, just out of eyesight, as the adults discussed a memory or a special someone from decades past. The tales were often exciting or funny. Others were serious or sad. The characters— so interesting! And they were all connected to me and my family!

I found out that my maternal grandmother's father was 61 years old when she was born. She said that when my great-grandfather was a child, he could recall holding his mother's hand, watching his older brothers in their Union blues marching off to fight in the Civil War. My imagination ran!

Fast forward a few decades, and my love of family stories has blossomed into a full-fledged career as a professional genealogist. Now, in addition to researching my own family history, I help other people learn more about their families' histories. This book is another way for me to help people learn about their ancestors and become effective stewards of their families' histories.

Why are people interested in family history?

People of all ages and backgrounds are flocking to the field of genealogy in ever-increasing numbers. What's behind the surge? I think the interest has always been there, but in recent years media and technology have changed the dynamics. Consider these factors:

➤ The widespread availability of inexpensive or free software for managing family records.

➤ Easier access to vital records and other data, thanks to online databases, social networks, and email.

➤ Television programs such as *History Detectives* and *Finding Your Roots,* which explain basic research concepts and share interesting genealogy stories involving famous people.

➤ Ever-present ads telling consumers how "easy" it is to trace your family tree.

Maybe you have seen the ads, or watched some of the TV programs. You may be very interested in learning about your own family tree. But where do you *really* start?

For me, genealogy is more than just a collection of names and dates. I went into the field because I want to know *who my ancestors were.* They may no longer be with us, but they are the reason I am here today. They were people, not just a bunch of names and dates listed in a dusty book or stored in a database. They had hopes, dreams, and needs, just as we all do. Through my research I am able to make connections, and watch personal stories unfold before me.

All kinds of people are interested in learning more about their roots. Do any of the following profiles seem familiar?

➤ **Sarah's grandmother always told her that the family came to North America on the *Mayflower,*** but no one ever seemed to believe the story. Curious, Sarah started to research her family history to see if her grandmother was right. Soon, she not only found one, but several *Mayflower* ancestors, and a fascinating family tree with roots across colonial New England. Thanksgiving now takes on a special meaning at her home. As she digs deeper into the family's history, the whole family loves learning about her discoveries.

➤ **John was adopted at birth and now wants to connect with his biological family.** Using what little information he knows about his origins, he has tried searching online and through paper records, but has not been able to find much. John has now turned to DNA testing with the hope that he can find a relative who will help him fill in his family tree and lead him to his birth parents.

➤ **Rose is of African-American heritage and wants to know more about the origins of her family.** Her grandparents did not talk much about growing up in Georgia, or about their extended families. Moreover, several records were destroyed in a house fire. Rose is certain that if she goes back far enough, she will find ancestors who were slaves. Nevertheless, she has a strong desire to know their stories.

➤ **David's father said the family's surname was changed at Ellis Island when their immigrant ancestor arrived in 1882.** After a visit to Ellis Island for a school trip, David discovered that the family legend was not supported by evidence in immigration records. Curious about why his great-grandfather, who was from Prussia, may have changed his name after arriving, David has begun to research his family history. He hopes one day he will be able to find records in Eastern Europe, where his family originated.

➤ **After Margaret's mother died, Margaret was cleaning out the attic.** She found a trunk full of letters, a family Bible, and old photographs. No one in the family recognizes the people in those photos, but Margaret noticed her mother's maiden name on the backs of several of the pictures. She has begun to reach out to cousins far and wide. One day she hopes to learn the identities of all of the people in the old photos, and where they came from.

Later, I will share more information about these cases. The names are not real, but the situations are based on real family research situations that can give you insights into your own genealogy quests.

What's in this guide

Genealogy has been around for hundreds of years in Europe. At first, it was a way for heralds to track noble families. At the end of the 19th Century, genealogy became a way for Americans to document their lineage—both Old World and Native American lines. In the 1970s, Alex Haley's *Roots* came to the small screen, energizing a new generation to seek out their family origins.

Genealogy is now booming. Thanks to an array of new tools and information sources, there has never been a better time to learn about your family's history. But the process can be daunting.

That's where this guide comes into play. This short guide will not only explain basic concepts and methods for family research, but it will also help you approach your research tasks in a smarter way that will save time and hopefully lead to better results. Topics include:

- ➤ The best approach to building a family tree and charting your research

- ➤ The most important records to look for

- ➤ Five things that can really trip up newbies (and tips for avoiding them)

- ➤ Dealing with "brick walls" in family research

- ➤ Approaching relatives for records, information, and family stories

- ➤ Research road trips, and what to bring in your portable genealogy kit

- ➤ The promise and perils of online research

- ➤ Getting started with genetic genealogy

- ➤ How to properly cite your findings

- ➤ Preserving family records and research for the next generation

We only have 30 minutes, so let's get started!

CHAPTER 1

Starting your family tree

You live as long as you are remembered.
—*Russian proverb*

You cannot build a tall building without a good foundation. The same is true of your family tree. Branches need a strong support system. This chapter covers the basic elements that you need to know to start building a tree that will not only make you proud, but will also inspire and educate your extended family and the generations that follow.

The starting point for any family history project

If you know someone who has conducted serious family research, take him or her aside and ask this simple question:

"Where do I begin?"

The answer won't be "online" or "the genealogy section at the local library." Rather, the advice should steer you to your own home. After all, you are the base of your family tree. Start with yourself, and then work backwards.

It seems simple, doesn't it? However, many novice researchers do not start with themselves at the base of the tree. Instead, they fly up into the branches, collecting data and entering names willy-nilly into an online genealogy database. The information they are entering may not even be accurate—it could be mixed up with someone else's information, or be based on a family legend Great-Aunt Agatha told them as a child.

Don't get me wrong. While family legends are interesting and inspiring, it's important to go about collecting and documenting data in a methodical way if the goal is to establish the facts and determine the true story of your ancestry.

PROTIP: Separating fact from myth in family stories

Stories are amazing and wonderful. They connect generations and let us relive moments in time with our ancestors. Unfortunately, they can also lead family researchers down the wrong paths. The more an old tale is passed around, the more likely it will contain mistakes, misunderstandings, or exaggerations. If your mother tells you a story about her grandmother, ask her who told her the story. If it was her grandmother retelling a story about her own life, it is a good bet that the story is mostly accurate. On the other hand, if it was a retelling late one night of a story her grandfather told her about his parents, well, it *might* be 100% accurate ... or it could be 10% accurate. People leave parts out, accidentally change small details, or in some instances, get the story completely wrong. This is why family stories should be used as clues in your family research, as opposed to factual accounts. Until you can prove the story actually happened, it's just a great story, and not proof of an event or relationship.

Another reason experienced genealogists tell novices to begin with themselves, and their own homes, is because it should be easier to locate critical documents to start the tree.

What kind of documents? Most people begin with their own birth and marriage certificates. It should be easy to dig out the same basic documents for your spouse and children. You may even have records for other family members, especially if you were involved with the estate of a relative, or if you inherited old family documents from someone.

There is another aspect of starting a tree that relates to recording what you know about yourself and close family members, including basic facts (names, dates of birth, etc.) and details relating to occupation, religion, places of residence, military service, and more. We will talk more about journaling in Chapter 4, but in the meantime keep in mind that such details can help inform you about the types of documents to seek out.

The importance of linking generations

Documents that link generations are crucial to building your tree. For instance, a birth certificate will link a child to his or her parents by listing all of their names, as well as information such as age and place of birth.

For your own tree, you can create links to your parents. Then move on to your grandparents, and so on. Do not move further back in time to the previous generation until it is possible to link a child to a parent or set of parents. It should be easy to get a government-issued birth, marriage, or death record for anyone in your family who was born in the past 100 years. These documents are great because they usually provide proof for connections to the previous generation.

Dig out your own birth or marriage certificate. Do you see where it lists your parents' names? Voila, a link to the past!

This may seem like a waste of time. After all, we know who our parents are, and probably our grandparents, too. Heck, some people even know or remember their great-grandparents. But what separates the casual researcher from the serious family historian is this: The serious family historian will take the time to gather the facts and documentation to prove the names and dates, even for close family members. The casual researcher may enter names and dates into a family tree, but won't bother to document his or her findings.

Here is another way of looking at the importance of linking generations: As a genealogist, you are not just documenting family history for yourself. You are doing it for other people, too. Your kids, grandchildren, nieces, nephews, cousins, or their descendants may turn to your research some day. They may not know how one generation links to another, so they will need to see these documented links in order to trust your research.

Bottom line: Take the time to link generations with documented facts. In Chapter 4, we will look at different ways to organize your records and make source citations. You (and your descendants) will thank you for your diligence later on!

Getting the right records

You may have heard the term *vital record* in the past. Vital records are created by the government and are usually considered official proof of an event. Vital records (government-issued birth, marriage, and death records) are the cornerstones of present- day genealogical research. However, non-vital records such as church records are also important, and at times may be easier to find. This section will cover the different types of records available to family researchers.

Vital records, from birth certificates to death certificates

Not all vital records are created equal. Different jurisdictions have often used different requirements for the types of information included in vital records. Some states in the U.S. gather quite a bit of information, whereas records from the U.K. or Canada seem sparse by comparison. Nevertheless, at a basic level, they should include:

➤ The date(s) of the event.

➤ The name of the person(s) for the event.

➤ The place where the event occurred.

Some vital records contain additional information, such as parents' names, maiden names, and other data. This is important, as we will learn later in this chapter.

Starting with your own vital records, you can begin your family tree with relative ease. You are person number one on your tree. Add in other members of your family who live with you and start their branches by gathering their documents as well.

Non-vital records and census forms

What if you can't find vital records? In the United States, vital records were not required in many states before the 20th Century. In some localities, vital records were kept starting at an earlier date, but may have been applied inconsistently. In addition, many vital records have been lost or destroyed over the years.

Overseas, the situation may be even worse. If you have to turn to records in another country, make a point of learning about the history of records and recordkeeping in that country.

Non-vital records consist of official records as well as religious records and other recorded information. They include:

➤ Census records

➤ Will/probate/estate records

➤ Church records

➤ Newspapers

Census records are the go-to resource for many families attempting to trace their roots. In the United States, the federal census has been taken every 10 years since 1790. (Some states, including New York, also conducted their own censuses in the late 1800s and early 1900s.) The U.K. started taking a census every ten years beginning in 1841, while the Canadian census was taken every ten years beginning in 1851.

The information gathered by census enumerators varied. Some early censuses only recorded names of the heads of each household, while others gathered detailed information about ages, occupations, and country of origin.

In the U.S., federal census records are released to the public 72 years after they are created. In 2012, the 1940 U.S. Census was released to much fanfare. Why all of the excitement? One reason relates to the fact that there are people living today who were children or young adults at the time of that census. The 1940 data can tell us many things about families, neighborhoods, and other relationships, and it can bring up fond memories (as well as good research material).

When the 1940 federal census came out, I sat down with my father and we went page by page through the census records for his old neighborhood. While he was only a toddler at the time, he could tell me about each family on his street. He showed me where his aunts and uncles lived. Then he told me who owned what store and who worked where. It was not only a trip down memory lane for him, but I was also able to fill out some branches on the family tree, plus get an insight into his hometown history.

PITFALL: Census errors

Sometimes census records may be the only government documentation you can find for a particular family. Unfortunately, census data can be wrong. Until the 1940 federal census, local census enumerators were not even required to document who supplied the information. The informant may have been the 13-year-old child who happened to answer the door, or perhaps the next-door neighbor if no one was home. This means that while the location of a family may be correct on a particular census record, names may be misspelled, and ages may be way off. Because of the likelihood of errors, always try to verify census records with vital records or information from other sources.

Estate records and newspaper articles

Estate records can be very enlightening, as many list family members and provide an easy way to link two generations. Finding the maiden names of maternal ancestors can be challenging, but wills often list a woman by her married name and identify her as a daughter of the deceased. Also, you can get a glimpse into the lifestyle of the family. By reading these documents, you can get a sense of:

➤ How much money/land they owned

➤ Property addresses

➤ Family priorities

➤ Family dynamics

Newspapers provide amazing insights into the social history of a particular time and place. Reading a newspaper written in the town in which your ancestor resided will really open your eyes to the community and climate of the era. Items of interest include:

➤ Community announcements

➤ News articles

➤ Trial coverage

➤ Gossip/society columns

➤ Work and school announcements

➤ Awards

➤ Local business announcements

➤ Announcements of births, marriages, and deaths

It's also fun to read the ads in old newspapers . . . I often find myself wishing that prices were still so low!

PITFALL: News reports involving ancestors

If an ancestor is mentioned in a newspaper article, it will be third parties—including reporters, editors, and proofreaders—who gathered and interpreted the information, and cut the story down to size. The article may not be 100% accurate, so fact-checking will be needed.

Religious records

Religious records can be hit or miss. A baptismal or marriage record can be a huge help when vital records or census data are not available. Even if your ancestor did not regularly attend religious services, he or she may have participated in services marking major life events, such as birth, baptism, marriage, or funeral.

However, religious records (especially those from the 18th Century and earlier) are inconsistent and may not be easily accessed. You will need to learn about your ancestor's religious denomination and determine what records have been preserved. The church, synagogue, or other congregation may not have records from a particular time period, or may restrict access. If you are able to locate such records, you may be able to determine:

➤ Name(s)

➤ Date of event

➤ Other family members present (parents, spouses)

➤ Witnesses (who may be friends or family)

What it feels like to run into a brick wall

Sooner or later it will happen to you. You're moving up your tree, filling in names and other information at a steady clip. And then—smack! You run face-first into a brick wall.

I'm not talking about a real brick wall, of course, but rather a research-related brick wall. Everyone runs into at least one brick wall when building a family tree, and some may seem impossible to break through.

For instance, when I was researching my husband's family, I tried to connect his great-great-grandmother to her parents. But there was a problem—the maiden name listed on her 1897 marriage certificate in New York City did not match other records.

Through persistent research I was able to scale the brick wall. It took two years, but I eventually unraveled the mystery. I determined that either she or her fiancé used her stepfather's surname as her maiden name on the marriage license. I determined her true surname after locating the marriage certificate drafted for her stepfather and mother in 1884. It listed her mother as a widow, and gave her maiden name and previous married name on the document. I was not able to move another generation back in time until that discovery was made.

Moral of the story: Don't give up if you hit a brick wall! In time, patience and dogged research may help you solve the mystery.

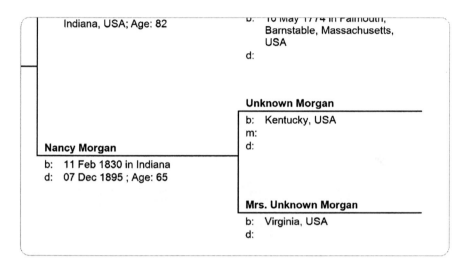

Five things that can trip up newbies researching family history

The next section is going to walk you through some of the common mistakes made by newbie and seasoned genealogists alike.

1. Danger! Wrong family ahead!

In the thrill of the hunt, it's possible to make mistakes. It happens to all of us. I actually traced the wrong Bennett family group for two years before I found the document that proved they were not related to my family. This illustrates an important lesson: It's OK to make mistakes. What matters most is that you identify and correct them.

2. Published genealogies and "tree rot"

Don't believe everything you read. Not everything that is in print is true, whether it's a book, a magazine article, or an online post. Published genealogies may also contain false information and conclusions based on incomplete data or wrong assumptions. In this field, new information is continually coming to light that may prove someone else's hard work was actually wrong.

Online family trees can be especially problematic. Many people simply click and add ancestors to their own trees without looking deeper into who the person was and the origins of the information used to build the source tree. This causes many errors to be passed from family tree to family tree in a process I call "tree rot." Someone makes a mistake and the error is propagated to other people's trees. I have seen entire lines merged into families who had no connection. These kinds of errors can lead to a lot of frustration and wasted time.

PROTIP: Working trees vs. official trees

You're hot on the trail of a mysterious ancestor. You have a name, a town, and a birth year. You dig into the local vital records and federal census data and then . . . two people turn up! They have the same name, the same birth year, and lived in the same town. So which person do you add to your official tree?

The answer: neither, at least not yet. Instead, you can resort to a "working tree" which contains your "maybe" research—research that will not be integrated into your official family tree. Create a file where you can gather information on the person(s) you are trying to prove for your family line. When you solve the identity issue with the potential ancestor, you can then add the collected documents and information to your official tree.

Always be skeptical of another person's research until you have completed the following steps:

➤ Check the person's sources. If that individual doesn't have any, treat the information as a potential clue, rather than an established fact (we will cover source citations in Chapter 4).

➤ Check the date. Sometimes older information is better because it was still fresh when it was gathered. On the other hand, genealogists from earlier periods often had laxer standards of research. Newer works with footnotes tend to be more trustworthy.

➤ Who was the publisher? If you have access to books published by a reputable source, such as the Mayflower family books by the General Society of Mayflower Descendants, you can be assured the resource is trustworthy. This organization (and others like it) will publish updates and new volumes as they become available so that amateur researchers will have access to accurate information in the future. Reputable genealogical publishers will frequently accept inquiries from readers.

3. Do the dates match up?

If you have a child in your tree who was born before his or her mother was born, you don't have a time-traveler on your hands. Rather, you have a problem. For whatever reason, incorrect data has found its way into the family history, and it's up to you to fix it.

These types of issues plague newbie genealogists. You have to be vigilant, and catch problems early in the research process. One best practice is to examine the birth, marriage, and death dates for each person in your tree before adding another one. If something looks wrong, make a note to follow up. If you have multiple possible dates for a single event, add them to your research notes. The problem could be a simple clerical error at the registry office 100 years ago, or it could be the result of trying to shoehorn someone into a tree where they don't belong.

4. It's Miller time!

A pox on everyone who has a common name! I have several "John Miller" lines in my family who happened to give their children the same names (John, Joseph, Mary, and Amelia). They were all good German Lutheran families, and this is how they named their children. I wanted to scream every time I had to try to sort out which of the 30 John Millers from a small farming community was *my* John Miller.

The only thing to do in these situations is to methodically go through each family until you find the proof that links the right person to your tree. It will take time, coffee, and a whole lot of patience!

5. Spelling variations

When digging into old vital records and census forms, don't be surprised to run into multiple spellings of someone's first or given names. It really wasn't until the 20th Century that the exact spelling of a person's name became important. In earlier eras, spelling was more fluid. Sometimes it was phonetic, particularly if it was a census taker speaking to an immigrant family who could not write or speak perfect English. The census worker would oftentimes make a best guess at a family name. There are instances where you can get a hint of a person's accent simply by looking at the way a clerk spelled his or her name on a document.

Let's look at an example. For my Combs ancestors, I have seen the surname for my great-great-great-great-grandfather (or fourth great-grandfather) Charles spelled the following ways:

➤ Coombs

➤ Combes

➤ Comes

➤ Coombes

➤ Comb

If you throw an immigrant into the mix, there can be even more options. For example, my German ancestor John Miller sometimes had his first name spelled Johann, Johannes, and Johnathan. His last name was spelled Mueller, Müller, or Mueler.

Case Study: Finding Sarah's connections to the *Mayflower*

Do you remember Sarah from the introduction, who looked into her family history after remembering her grandmother's stories about being descended from passengers on the *Mayflower*? She began her journey just like every other family genealogist. She started at the base of the tree (herself) and worked her way back through time to establish the connection to the *Mayflower* and the colony established at Plymouth in 1620.

First, Sarah gathered the documents pertaining to herself, her husband, and her children. Then, she visited her mother, who was so happy that Sarah was interested in learning more about her heritage. Her mother spent an entire weekend with Sarah, digging out old papers and telling stories. By the time Sarah left her mother's home, she had crucial documents for her mother, her father, and a few of her grandparents.

After these relatively easy steps were taken to establish the base of her tree, it was time to flesh out the branches. Sarah knew that if she was going to prove grandma right concerning the *Mayflower* connection, she had to work her way back carefully. Online research helped her go back four more generations, to the early 1800s. Next, she went to the local library and looked at the books in their genealogy collection. The librarian helped her start her search and gave her pointers on what she should do next.

There were a few missteps along the way, but eventually she researched far enough back to connect a great-great-great-great grandfather to an official lineage published by the Mayflower Society. Quickly, her family tree opened up before her eyes, and she could not believe her luck as two additional lines were connected to *Mayflower* descendants. Months of research had paid off and she proved that her grandmother was correct after all!

CHAPTER 2

Genealogy road trips

Do you not know that a man is not dead while his name is still spoken?
—Terry Pratchett

In the last chapter, I told you that your journey in search of your family history begins with you. Hopefully you are ready to scour your house and your memory for the clues to document your family history. This chapter will build on that basic foundation by teaching you how to gather information from all kinds of sources. Think of it as somewhat like constructing a building:

1. You lay the foundation with good principles and techniques.

2. Then, you find the bricks, which are the documents you gathered.

3. Next, you add floors as you delve back in time through your history, placing one brick and then another brick.

4. And, of course, you decorate each floor as you go, with the stories, pictures, and the details of the people's lives who came before you.

Once again, we will start this process at home with ourselves, but I will also discuss online and onsite repositories. Contrary to popular belief, not all genealogy records are online. Many experts estimate that less than a quarter of the records that are relevant to genealogical research are currently online.

Where are the other records? Some are in people's homes. Others are in institutions such as churches, town halls, libraries, and federal repositories. You can find information in cemeteries, too. Keep this in mind as you conduct your research. At some point on your genealogical journey, you will have to venture away from close family sources and your computer.

The great family document hunt

After combing your attic, basement, and closets for documents that can help you build your family tree, it's time to expand the search to your relatives' homes. They may have vital records, family letters, photographs, and other papers that can fill out your tree or verify data that you have already collected.

Before you contact relatives, prepare a list what you are looking for. In the first pass through Great-Aunt Millicent's house, you are primarily looking for documents, although she may insist on passing you boxes of old photos, an antique clock, and a tuna casserole. While the things she gives you may be great finds and fantastic gifts, stay focused on getting documents on your first visit. Unless you are traveling a great distance, you can always come back for a second visit.

What kind of documents? Anything that can establish identities, link generations, and expand your tree. In other words, you are looking for vital records and other documents that show names, dates, and places. This information can also be used to fill out a basic pedigree chart (see Chapter 4) for your family.

Here is a short list of documents to look for:

➤ Birth/marriage/death certificates

➤ Letters

➤ Wills

➤ Diplomas

➤ Military records

➤ School records

➤ Employment records

➤ Diaries

➤ Journals

➤ Handwritten family trees

Don't just ask immediate relatives—go for cousins, too. Relatives several generations removed may have records that you do not. When someone dies, it is quite common for the estate to be divided among different family members. You can never be too sure who has an important piece of family history boxed up in a closet or attic.

It is important to interview older relatives. They are one or two steps closer to the past than you are. The stories you capture in interviews with them will not only add color and life to your family tree, but may also reveal clues to puzzles you are trying to solve.

When I started my family research, I called my parents and warned them that I would be combing the house for records and documents when I next visited. My mom and dad were very helpful and pulled out shoeboxes, albums, and large plastic totes from the recesses of their home so I could paw through 100 years of family records. My husband and kids pitched in—we had a great time going through it all together.

I took lots of notes and asked lots of questions. I wrote down family stories and the background of various objects and heirlooms. The effort made for some great memories and it really kicked me into high gear for expanding the research into my ancestors.

PITFALL: Compiled genealogies

More than once, someone has told me that I don't need to work on my family history because it has already been published in a book. However, just because the information is in print does not mean it is accurate. The genealogy may be for a different branch of the family. It could be hopelessly outdated, or filled with information that is based on hearsay. Citations are key—if no sources are listed, be very cautious about the accuracy of the text.

"You are wasting your time!"

Not all family members will be so keen to help. There are relatives who may not want to share information. Some may even tell you that you are wasting your time and the past should be left in the past.

It can be very frustrating to deal with negative people. Nevertheless, when it comes to family history, I have found that givers far outnumber the keepers. If you get the cold shoulder from Uncle Bob, don't try to convince him to let you take something he is not comfortable parting with. Move on to the next family connection ... but keep open the possibility of coming back. Over time, trust may be established. Once Uncle Bob understands that you will care for a particular record, he may let you have more freedom with his collection.

PROTIP: Building trust

Have you ever heard the old saying that it's easier to catch flies with honey than vinegar? Well, when it comes to dealing with family, you may need to be your sticky-sweetest! This particularly holds true when talking with older generations of your family. They may still regard you as the little kid playing outside on the swing and may not take you seriously. Take it in stride, but remember that you are asking them to share mutual family history. When a distant relative does welcome you in to look through old documents or other records, be gracious. Being polite and thankful is a sure-fire way to get invited back if and when the relative finds something new.

As the youngest in my generation, I frequently run into distrustful relatives. A dear great aunt of mine told me a few years ago that I should get my head out of the clouds with this genealogy nonsense and worry about making a good home for my babies. But her attitude eventually changed. Two visits later, she was pulling out bags of newspaper clippings (she clipped everything about the family for 60 years) and tubs of old textiles so I could see items from my great-grandparents' home. It just took patience on my part and time for her to realize this was not a passing fancy!

What to include in a portable genealogy kit

If I know I am going to a relative's house, library, or other location to conduct genealogy research, I reach for my portable genealogy kit. It contains tools to gather clues and take notes, including:

- ➤ Smartphone for taking photos, recording interviews, and accessing genealogy apps

- ➤ Camera and/or portable scanner (if no smartphone is available)

- ➤ Small notebook or electronic tablet

- ➤ Pencil and/or archive-safe pens

- ➤ Small ruler (clear rulers are best)

- ➤ Post-it notes

- ➤ USB flash drive for transferring computer files

- ➤ Paper clips

- ➤ Rubber bands

- ➤ ID/access/payment cards for libraries, copiers, etc.

Smartphone cameras and apps

The first item on the list is a smartphone. A good smartphone can be an invaluable tool for gathering information when visiting a relative's house, a cemetery, or some other genealogical site.

The camera on a new smartphone is as good, if not better, than the old digital camera that might be lying in a desk drawer. It can be used to take pictures of people, documents, buildings, or gravestones. You can use the smartphone's video capabilities to record interviews or tours of family properties. Propping up the camera to shoot a video interview is less intrusive than taking notes during our conversations. In addition, the family will treasure being able to share the video with future generations.

The audio recorder app can be used to record interviews or your own dictations. Use a note-taking app to jot down important pieces of information.

I also like to use my phone's video option when I am talking with older family members. If you are not comfortable with taking pictures or video with your phone or digital camera, make a point of learning how to use the various features before you go on a genealogical expedition.

There is a wide variety of apps geared toward genealogy research. Most of the major online genealogy services have apps that let members access family trees and online databases while on the go. Accessing the data is not just for your benefit—imagine being able to whip out your phone and show Aunt Millicent an up-to-date version of your family tree!

Other electronics

If your phone is old or otherwise not suitable for a heavy-duty genealogy road trip, you can bring along other types of electronics. A standard digital camera can be used to photograph anything relatives are unable or unwilling to part with, from papers to paintings. I also carry a small portable printer/scanner if I think I might need to make a lot of paper copies or scan documents. You can find a decent portable printer/scanner for about $100 at most office supply stores. The one I use has a flash memory card, which I can take out and insert into my laptop to offload the images.

Regardless of the type of devices you bring with you, remember to pack power supplies, such as charging cables, plugs, and batteries. You never want to run out of power halfway through your research. Clamshell cases for eyeglasses are wonderful for transporting cables and plugs and preventing them from getting tangled with other items.

Taking notes

You will take notes—lots of notes! Sometimes my parents will say something when we are sitting at the kitchen table and I have to stop them so I can jot down what I just heard. It may be a story I have never heard before, a new name, an event, or something else. My notebook or tablet is never far away from me. As the "builder" of the family history, I need to collect all those scraps for the structure I am creating.

PROTIP: Other items for your genealogy kit

Genealogy researchers prefer to use pencils over pens because they are less damaging to paper records, photographs, and other items. In addition, many archives and libraries will not let visitors use pens in their research areas. If you do bring pens in your kit, I suggest you invest in a few different colors that use archival-quality ink. Unlike the acidic ink found in most regular pens, archival-quality pens won't bleed or damage paper. My portable genealogy kit also includes erasers, a small ruler (to measure photos or other objects), sticky notes, and a USB flash drive to copy digital images stored on computers or other devices.

How to protect and transport documents and photos

The National Archives in Washington, D.C. used to hold an onsite genealogy fair. The first time I attended, it was held outside on Pennsylvania Avenue on a wet, cold, and miserable March day. I huddled with some friends around the booths, avoiding the drips and trying to listen to lectures through chattering teeth. By the time I got home, everything I gathered was limp and wet. While it was just fliers and brochures (as opposed to important research documents), I learned that it's important to be prepared for anything on a genealogy-related excursion!

We will cover different ways to label genealogy materials and prepare them for long-term storage in Chapter 5. For the time being, you need to think about how to keep your documents and other family items safe on the way home from your genealogy road trip. Storing your materials improperly can lead to their demise. In the past few decades, a lot of new archival-safe products have come on the market, thanks to the scrapbooking craze. Take advantage of them, and ensure that you store your papers and photos in a way that will protect them for several more generations.

When I travel for research, I bring sturdy plastic folders or accordion folders with me. These are a great way to keep photocopies and other materials clean, safe, and organized until you return home where you can examine them more carefully. They will also not get creased or crumpled if you are flying.

General guidelines for storing and transporting important papers, photos, and other materials include:

➤ Invest in acid-free products (document sleeves, paper, boxes, etc.).

➤ Store large items in boxes in temperature-controlled locations (such as interior closets of your home, as opposed to attics and basements).

➤ Place documents in clear plastic sleeves inside binders or folders.

➤ Always have multiple backups of paper and digital images.

Remember, it's important to take the long view when it comes to gathering records and documenting the family history. Key resources need to be available for future generations to learn from. A copy of the church record you retrieved from your ancestral home may be the only one in existence should a disaster hit the church's archive.

PROTIP: Filing follies

One of the hardest things to do when returning from a research trip is making the time to file away all of the goodies you found. The papers I gather during research trips can sit in piles or bags for weeks before I get around to actually putting them where they belong. It's a bad habit, not only because it leads to clutter, but also because details about certain documents may be forgotten or misplaced. We will cover how to organize and preserve physical records in chapters 4 and 5.

Case Study: David's Ellis Island mystery

In high school, David made a trip to Ellis Island with his social studies class to learn about the history of European immigration in the 1800s and early 1900s. For David, it was more than a school field trip to a famous New York City landmark. Some of David's forebears had come through the immigrant processing center in New York harbor more than 100 years before. He imagined his great-grandfather walking down the gangplank onto the docks and into the giant arrival hall. David got chills when he thought about walking in his footsteps.

David's father claimed their surname had been changed at Ellis Island, perhaps by a harried clerk. But a ranger at Ellis Island, which is now part of a national park, told David this was highly unlikely.

David was intrigued and decided to learn more about his Ellis Island ancestors. David started his research at the National Archives at New York City. The archive holds the naturalization records for millions of immigrants. David hoped to determine the real story. The research trip yielded all he was looking for, and more. By looking at the naturalization records, he learned where his great-grandfather came from in Eastern Europe, when he arrived, his birth date, and most importantly, his actual name.

The information helped David fill out his tree, and eventually find cousins all over the United States. In the near future, he plans a research trip with his family to Eastern Europe to visit his ancestral village. David plans to hire a local researcher to help him translate documents and learn more about the history of the village. If he is lucky, he may even find other living cousins!

CHAPTER 3

Online research, genetic genealogy, and other resources

History remembers only the celebrated, genealogy remembers them all.
—*Laurence Overmire*

Have you ever seen the advertisements for online genealogy services? The slickest ones suggest you can simply log in, enter a few names, and your family tree will magically unfold before your eyes.

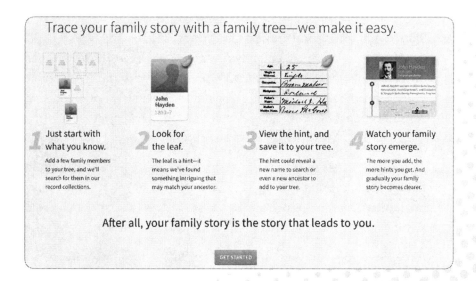

Trace your family story with a family tree—we make it easy.

1 Just start with what you know.

Add a few family members to your tree, and we'll search for them in our record collections.

2 Look for the leaf.

The leaf is a hint—it means we've found something intriguing that may match your ancestor.

3 View the hint, and save it to your tree.

The hint could reveal a new name to search or even a new ancestor to add to your tree.

4 Watch your family story emerge.

The more you add, the more hints you get. And gradually your family story becomes clearer.

After all, your family story is the story that leads to you.

GET STARTED

For most people, the journey to discovering family origins is never so easy, even with high-tech tools. There are millions of people who may go years without ever knowing about anyone older than their grandparents. It really depends on what documents are available and the self-education you put into discovering your roots.

That said, it *is* easy to get started. Anyone can fire up a web browser and enter some names and dates into an online database. It is also possible to create an online family tree, or use desktop genealogy software to track various branches of your family. But there are also potential pitfalls to using these tools:

➤ **Online tools encourage casual searches.** Remember the outline for family research, given in Chapter 1? The idea is to start at the base of the tree (you and your immediate family) and then work back by linking generations. However, it can be so tempting to skip all of that and start entering unverified names into online databases to see what turns up. It can lead you down false paths. You may end up wasting a lot of time.

➤ **There is a learning curve associated with using new digital tools.** Even if you have used online genealogy services in the past, a new service may not have the same features or may use a different interface.

➤ **Sensitive information may be unwittingly shared.** Many online services encourage users to upload or create family trees. However, some of them make the trees (and the data associated with them) visible to other members or the public by default. This may be an important consideration if sensitive family details or relationships are involved.

➤ **Services may not be able to talk with each other.** Let's say you have an extensive tree on Service A. You discover Cousin Francine has built out an obscure branch of the family on Service B. You need the data, but it turns out there is no easy way to share it other than copying and pasting names and source citations from a report she generates.

➤ **Genealogy software and online services are not always free.** Paying a monthly or annual fee for access to online databases is typical. If you keep the subscription going for years, it can get expensive.

Crossing the paper/digital divide

The paper/digital divide can be formidable. When you put out a call to your extended family letting them know you are gathering information about your forebears, do not be surprised when you start receiving information in the form of boxes containing hundreds of papers from family genealogists who have conducted research the old-fashioned way. Bringing paper-based data into the digital world will require lots of effort and care.

The paper/digital divide can manifest itself in other ways. For instance, you may want to grant your relatives access to your digital tree at some point. But what if they are not proficient computer users, or don't have the right type of software to examine it?

The paper/digital divide can also lead to frustration when conducting research at libraries, government offices, or other institutions. You may want to use digital cameras, scanners, laptops, and other devices to record data and take notes. But the rules may state that cameras are forbidden, they don't take emailed requests, and you must pay $1 per page at the copy machine.

The point is, you need to be flexible. After you pick the low-hanging fruit online, you may need to drag out a ladder to get to the higher fruit that may not be located online . . . and then undertake additional work to bring everything back into the digital world.

PROTIP: The Golden Rule

Good behavior extends to strangers you come into contact with in the course of your research. If you know you will be regularly working with a particular repository, treat the staff nicely. When you talk with someone in person, online, or in an email, be gracious and treat him or her with respect. You would be surprised how a little politeness will help you go a long way.

Where to start online searches

There are hundreds of online databases available to family genealogists. Some are very broad, covering many countries and different types of vital and non-vital records. Others are narrowly focused on a certain region or family line.

Although the paid services will try to get you to sign up for a subscription, you can often access the more well-known services for free at libraries or a local Family History Center.

Popular paid services	Popular free services
Ancestry (*ancestry.com*)	Geni (*geni.com*)
Find My Past (*findmypast.com*)	FamilySearch (*familysearch.org*)
My Heritage (*myheritage.com*)	

Sometimes the simplest of solutions can give you the best payouts. Outside of dedicated genealogy websites, you can also find numerous clues to your heritage with a simple query on Google. More than once, a search for a surname, location, and sometimes a date or other detail has returned pages of results. The leads included links to old newspaper articles, cemetery lists, and other documents that contained clues about a branch of my tree. Try it yourself!

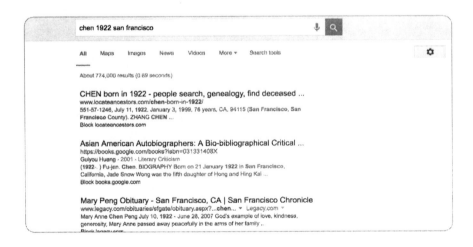

Finding gold in genealogy blogs

Since the early 2000s, tens of millions of individuals have created blogs around hobbies or other interests. Guess what: There are genealogy blogs as well! The vast majority of people who write genealogy blogs are not only doing so to document their research, but are also posting their findings in hopes of some-day being contacted by a distant relative who has stumbled upon their posts. So-called "cousin bait" includes names, fragments of trees, relevant documents, and analysis. Such blogs can provide information that would otherwise take years to find on your own, including family letters and photographs.

If you find such a blog that contains information about shared ancestors, be sure to reach out to the author for the rest of the story, which may include additional details or source citations. In addition, save a copy of the information in case the site disappears later.

The dangers of random searching

When I started my genealogy journey, I had so much fun just sitting at my computer after my kids were asleep or at school. I would sit in front of the screen for hours, happily saving, printing, and reading page after page of information about my family—or people with family surnames who *could* be in my family tree. My husband jokingly told friends that I liked to collect dead people.

I have a background in science and understand the principles of good research. However, when it came to family history, I was on a wild ride. I ended up throwing all caution to the wind. The hangover came a week later, when I was unable to determine the valid information among all of the useless stuff I had dug up.

What I experienced is actually an all-too-common occurrence among new genealogists. I like to call it the "research high." You have to follow just one more hint or clue or record before you can call it a night!

Why do this? Uncovering information is an addiction. If you happen to find the right clue or piece of evidence, it's like hitting the jackpot. After hours or days or months of research into a particular branch of your tree, it is an exciting thrill to be able to make a discovery and watch all the pieces of your puzzle fall into place. I once squealed in delight in the quiet reading room of the National Archives in Washington, D.C. Thankfully I was surrounded by people who understood and celebrated my discovery with me!

PITFALL: The thrill of the hunt . . . and the regret when it's over

An exciting research high based on willy-nilly online searches comes with a price that leaves most people flustered. A hot lead can turn into a multifaceted mystery, and you can also find yourself going in several directions at once. When you finally shut down the browser, you will have no idea how you got to that page or even what you were looking for two or three hours earlier. You end up chasing your tail, researching the same items, places, and people over and over again. Talk about a waste of time! That's why it is important that even when you are hot on an ancestor's trail, you should make sure you log your information and document your discoveries as you find them. In Chapter 4, we will discuss journaling and other techniques for documenting research.

Genealogy communities and continuing education

Genealogy is a field of study primarily based on self-education. But don't feel that you are completely alone. Local genealogy societies, books, conferences, webinars, and courses can connect you with like-minded people while helping you learn to be a better genealogist. You can further narrow the focus by learning about a specific country or time period that is important to your family. If you go down this road, you will never stop learning as a family historian.

We have covered many of the research basics so far, but there is a lot more out there. We can't delve into every option in less than 30 minutes, but the following information provides a glimpse into some of the other research and educational routes you may want to pursue.

Genealogy societies

Genealogy societies are groups of people who share a love and passion for genealogy research. There are local, regional, state, and national societies that can provide generic genealogy help as well as assistance for specific topics. Often there are educational workshops, lectures, or symposiums sponsored by the groups to help members hone their skills. There are a number of societies that focus on state research, ethnic groups, and other niches such as forensics. Most groups have regular meetings, and with many groups provide ways for members who live far away to participate using new technologies.

Lineage societies

Lineage societies are groups of people who have common ties through their family tree to someone who lived at a specific time or participated in an event. For instance, The Daughters of the American Revolution (DAR) are women who descend from someone who rendered aid to the Colonies during the American Revolution. That person may have been a soldier, or someone who gave money, provided supplies, or was part of an allied force.

Many people like to take their hours of research and apply to one of the hundreds of lineage societies out there. It is a great way to show others how good a researcher you are as well as give you a bit of bragging rights. You did a lot of work! Show it off and be proud. If lineage societies interest you, be sure to check out The Hereditary Society Community of the United States of America website, which has an extensive list of societies.

Conferences and seminars

Conferences and seminars are a great way to network with other people while learning about new techniques and research stories. A few of the larger national conferences are now live-streaming sessions for those people who cannot travel to the physical events. Some presentations are free but other sessions may require remote users to purchase a track of classes to watch from home. Many presentations end up on YouTube after the event is over.

Online forums

There are a number of websites and forums devoted to surnames or surname branches. Besides being able to ask and answer questions, members can also share their own research stories. Some forums exist on Facebook, too.

Webinars

Webinars are a great form of distance learning. While many organizations offer free online lectures to registered members, sites such as Legacy Family Tree Webinars and Family Tree University offer online lectures for anyone to purchase. Topics vary and cover everything from basic methodology to advanced and more obscure topics.

Genetic genealogy basics

In the past 10 years, a scientific revolution has swept the genealogy field. It's now possible for anyone to take a relatively inexpensive DNA test and match the results online against other people to determine if they are close relations, cousins, or more distant relatives.

Genetic genealogy tests look at your chromosomes, which are made up of extremely long Deoxyribonucleic Acid (DNA) molecules. A copy of your chromosomes can be found in every cell of your body. Most people have 23 chromosome pairs, including the 23rd pair which determines gender:

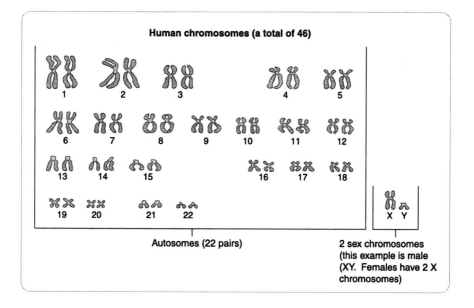

What is DNA? It is a code that is akin to a very detailed recipe. It determines gender, physical traits, and gives operating instructions for cell functions. Autosomal DNA is inherited from your parents, half coming from your mother and half from your father. An older or younger sibling also inherits DNA from your parents, but it will be a different mix. This explains the differences in physical traits between siblings (identical twins share the same DNA, though).

Genetic genealogy has been a boon to researchers trying to break through brick walls as well as ordinary people who want to know more about their origins. For some adoptees and orphans who have no paper records to turn to, DNA tests offer the only hope to reconnect with blood relatives.

Going back in time, you will share roughly 25% of your DNA with a grandparent. A first cousin will also share DNA with the same grandparent, which means that you and the cousin will have a certain percentage of shared DNA. Genetic genealogy services match more distant cousins by finding identical segments of DNA in the samples (usually saliva) provided by each person.

Taking a DNA test for genealogy is a personal decision. Your reasons may be different from the person sitting next to you, but the common thread is usually a desire to know more about family origins. It's also important to remember DNA testing is a tool, just like a census record. Coupled with other genealogical research, test results can help validate possibilities. DNA has led to more than one person confirming a hunch or proving a connection.

Different types of genetic tests

There are three types of DNA tests:

1. The Autosomal DNA (atDNA) test covers two areas. Also known as admixture DNA, atDNA is the non-sex-determining chromosomes located in the nucleus of a person's cells. From the same test, companies can also give results for the X chromosome. Men inherit one X chromosome from their mother. They then pass on that chromosome intact to their daughters. When combined with the atDNA results,

it's possible to narrow down which side of the family certain genetic information comes from.

2. Mitochondrial DNA (mtDNA) helps people trace their maternal lineage. Mitochondria are passed on to all children from their mothers. They are considered the "powerhouse of the cell" because they are the organelle that is responsible for producing energy for cell functions. These organelles contain their own DNA, which is separate and does not combine with the atDNA.

3. Y chromosome DNA (yDNA) tests are only available to men. They test the Y chromosome found in all males. It traces a direct paternal line back in time, which can help connect people with the same (or similar) surnames.

Private companies offer genetic genealogy tests. They include Family Tree DNA (FTDNA), 23andMe, Ancestry DNA (a service of *Ancestry.com*), and the National Geographic Genographic Project. To help members of the public make informed decision about the services provided by the different companies, Dr. Tim Janzen has created a DNA Test Comparison Chart on the International Society of Genetic Genealogy wiki, available at *isogg.org* . If you are interested in taking a test, visit a service provider's website to register and order kits.

Haplogroups: Your deep ancestral heritage

Many people take genetics genealogy tests because they want to determine where their ancestors came from. Haplogroup identification uses yDNA tests (for your paternal line) or mtDNA tests (for your maternal line) to determine deep ancestral heritage. By comparing your DNA against a list of known genetic mutations dating from thousands of years in the past, the tests can determine your paternal and maternal haplogroup branches, which are genetic populations associated with certain regions. For example, yDNA haplogroup F arose in South Asia. It is the parent of all yDNA haplogroups G through R, which trace back to various areas in Europe, the Middle East, and Asia. This includes yDNA haplogroup I, which arose in Europe thousands of years later.

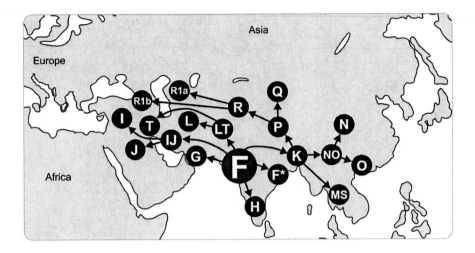

In some cases, mutations can be correlated with specific regions or even surnames. For those who do not know who their parents are, or where their ancestors immigrated from, haplogroups can help fill in the holes of their ancestral knowledge. However, note that ethnicity results are only estimates. Test providers make slightly different predictions due to the different control groups they use. Plus, the results that do show up only reflect the DNA you inherited. So, just because your great-great-grandmother's German genes are not represented in the results, doesn't mean she isn't your ancestor. It just means you did not inherit enough of those markers to show up in the test.

Finding skeletons in the genetic closet

While interpreting results can be difficult, DNA does not lie. Sometimes the tests unearth skeletons hiding in long-forgotten closets. A non-paternal event (NPE) is one of the most common surprises revealed through DNA testing. In a nutshell, NPEs are situations in which a parent/child does not match up with the expected lineage. An NPE could occur for many reasons:

➤ Undocumented name changes and/or aliases

➤ Incorrect family tree information or poor research

➤ A family trying to cover an illegitimate birth

➤ Hidden adoptions, foundlings, and previous marriages

➤ Affairs

If the NPE occurred several generations back, the paper trail may be difficult (or impossible) to resolve. For example, in my husband's family, one of his great-grandfathers changed his entire name in the mid-1860s to make a break with his past and start a new life in the American West. A DNA test of different branches would have established a relationship. However, had I not already uncovered this information from my research, the family connection would be unknown because the surnames would not match. In other words, it would have been a brick wall.

I have another example from my own family. My great-great-grandmother had a child out of wedlock at 18 with a local schoolteacher. When she married someone else four years later, the male child was taken in by her husband as his own and took his surname. It wasn't until after they were both dead that the family learned the oldest child had not really been his. In both instances, if male descendants were to undergo yDNA testing, they would not match the other male descendants of my great-great-grandmother.

Consumer protections under the GINA Act

Many people refuse to take DNA tests because they are afraid that insurance companies, the government, or their employer may be able to use that information against them. Thanks to the *Genetic Information Nondiscrimination Act (GINA) of 2008*, in the U.S. the only people who have access to DNA test results are the customers themselves and others who they grant permission to. Employers and insurance companies cannot access this information. Some other countries have adopted similar laws, but protections are by no means universal.

PITFALL: Genetic genealogy and pushy relatives.

When you are hot on the trail of a genealogy mystery, you may get very excited about potential discoveries through DNA tests. There may be a temptation to get everyone in the family on board ... right now! The rush to get people tested has led to a phenomenon of pushy DNA collectors who attempt to strong-arm relatives into handing over samples of their saliva.

Asking for a genetic sample is in a different league than asking relatives to share paper records. Moreover, it is rude. When you ask a relative to take a genetic genealogy test, you are asking that person to agree to giving up a piece of him or herself to a company. While you may offer to pay for the test, the results do not belong to you. They belong to the person who is providing the DNA. That person is simply allowing you to see the results. That person also has the right to say "no" if he or she does not wish to participate.

Case Study: An adoptee's story

John, an adoptee, loves his mom and dad. He was adopted as a baby, and they have been amazing parents, but there has always been a nagging question in the back of his mind: Who am I?

John was unable to locate any information about his birth parents because his records were sealed. Recently, he decided to turn to DNA testing.

Initially, John didn't know what he was doing. He tested at all of the major companies, but the results were confusing. John joined an online forum whose members include adoptees who have also taken DNA tests. Online, the members give each other support, and help guide new members. A few people explained John's test results to him.

After six months, John finally connected with a cousin who used one of the same genetic testing services. His cousin is so helpful. She shared her family tree with him and started to help him build his own tree online. Slowly the connections have grown, to the point where he thinks he knows who his birth mother is. He wants to make contact, but he also wants to be sure. More research needs to be done, but soon he hopes to solve the mystery and find out who he really is.

CHAPTER 4

Tracking and sharing your research

It takes as much energy to wish as it does to plan.
—Eleanor Roosevelt

We have touched on many aspects of conducting genealogical research, from the "whys" of genealogy to effective research techniques and common pitfalls. But there is another layer we need to discuss—how to keep track of it all.

Tracking includes everything from creating good source citations to outputting data to a chart or tree. Along with preserving research (which we will cover in Chapter 5), it's one of my least favorite tasks. After the initial excitement of making easy discoveries, it's so frustrating to deal with tracking and filing and storing all of the information and papers you have found.

On the other hand, charts and other summary documents are a great way to share findings to family members. When you bring a complete pedigree chart to a family reunion, it will attract attention and prompt lots of questions. Be sure to bring copies to give away!

This chapter will help you learn some tried and true techniques associated with tracking research. It's up to you, though, to maintain the discipline that you will need to be successful. If you have read this far, I am sure you are up for the challenge.

Visualizing family history with charts

The first project I made as a new genealogist was a family tree for my parents and in-laws. After a year of research on my lines and those of my husband, I was confident enough to put the names and dates to paper showing six generations of our family.

Family trees are fun to look at and serve as useful references for understanding basic relationships. But trees are just the tip of the iceberg when it comes to collating and maintaining the fruits of your research. Below are examples of pedigree charts, fan charts, and other basic chart types you can use to document your ancestors and track your research.

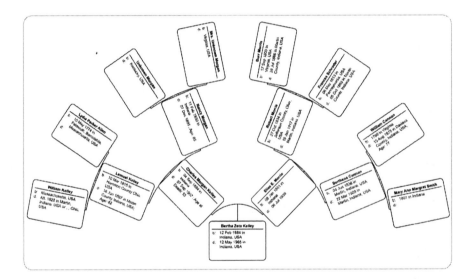

While many beginner genealogists (and even some pros) like working things out on paper, all genealogy software programs have print options for various types of trees and charts. In addition, it's useful to print out smaller sections when visiting relatives, or to use for jotting down notes when conducting research.

Digital vs. paper

How do you like to work? If you are comfortable with computers and software applications, the digital route may be appealing. On the other hand, sometimes the portability and permanence of paper calls to people.

PITFALL: Paper avalanche!

Should you decide to maintain paper charts, you will quickly accumulate reams of paper records. Keeping paper records also requires some sort of indexing system to reference people, family lines, charts, and other data. In the first year of research, I traced several lines back 10 generations, including children, spouses, and other members of collateral lines. There were several thousand people in all! Without a system to locate and keep track of everyone, I would have quickly lost people in the shuffle. In Chapter 5, we will discuss filing systems for paper records.

Whether you decide to keep track of your information digitally or on paper, templates and standardized forms are a huge help. We genealogists love neat, tidy, and ordered forms. A simple search will land you with all types of variations on the forms we are going to talk about in this section. The following online resources contain printable or downloadable forms that I find helpful:

➤ Cyndi's List (*cyndislist.com*)

➤ Family Tree Magazine (*familytreemagazine.com*)

➤ GenealogySearch.org (*genealogysearch.org*)

➤ National Archives (*archives.gov*)

➤ Family Search (*familysearch.org*)

If you can't find one you need, make your own. In addition, the companion website to this guide contains several downloadable forms at *genealogy. in30minutes.com*.

The standard pedigree chart

A pedigree chart is based on the classic family tree. It is the most common type of genealogy chart. Starting with yourself, a standard pedigree chart contains five generations. This is a great way to see, at a glance, the basic structure of your family tree. It contains the names and dates for each person and shows direct lineages. I always tell people who work with paper to fill this chart out in pencil. It is a worksheet and you will update the form with new information as you find it. Changing a date is much easier if it is in pencil. You can also use genealogy software and online services to generate pedigree charts.

Pedigree charts include a useful numbering system. Blank pedigree charts included in books or posted on the Internet come pre-numbered. If you are starting a pedigree chart for the first time, this is how you would write the information:

➤ You will be on the number 1 line

➤ Your father will be number 2

➤ Your mother will be number 3

➤ Grandparents are 4–7

➤ Great grandparents are 8–15

Did you notice any pattern? All male ancestors on the pedigree chart have even numbers, while female ancestors have odd numbers. In the Appendix, there is a sample pedigree chart demonstrating the numbering system.

If you are using paper, what happens when you get to the last line and you have more people to write down? The solution is simple: Start a new page. For example, let's say you want to continue with your paternal line, and you know several more generations past your paternal great-great-grandfather (that is, a second great grandfather), who is number 16 on the chart. On a new pedigree chart, place ancestor #16 in the number one position and begin filling out a new chart showing his direct line ancestry.

I also put a reference number on each page. Why? Because it is so easy to create dozens of pedigree charts for various branches of the family in a short amount of time. Here is the system I use:

➤ The chart with my name is page 1

➤ Starting with person #16, I create pages for each person on the last row of ancestors starting with page 2, where person #16 is the primary person

➤ For additional sheets, I add a letter. (For example, person #16 on page 2 would get his or her own chart with the reference number 2a.)

➤ Person 16 on page 2a could be labeled 2a1

As you can see, this can get complicated as more branches are added and you go further back in time. For this reason, you may want to invest in family tree software which can automatically fill in pedigree charts and other forms.

Variations of pedigree charts

There are other types of pedigree charts that present family relations in an easy-to-understand format. They include:

➤ **Fan chart.** This looks like a segmented half or full circle with one person in the center. Maternal ancestors appear on one half, and paternal ancestors on the other half (see image below).

➤ **Bow tie.** starting with a person in the center of the chart, the chart shows paternal ancestors on the left, and maternal ancestors on the right

➤ **Hourglass.** Starting with a person in the center of the chart, ancestors appear above this person and descendants appear below them.

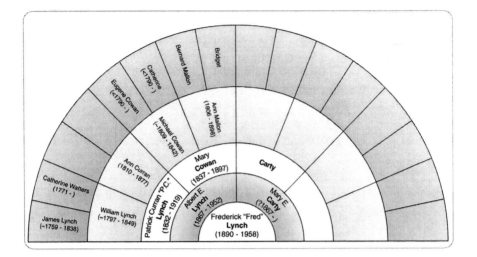

Many genealogy software programs let users generate standard pedigree charts or other formats, such as fan charts. Check the list of features or help resources for specific programs to understand what's available.

Family group sheet or family record

This document records detailed information about a specific family. At the top of the family group sheet are the parents and their vital information, followed by their children and their vital information. It is a crucial form for your research because you can view entire families at once, which allows you to see patterns emerge and identify holes in your knowledge.

Besides the parents and children's names, it also records:

➤ Dates of birth, marriage, and death

➤ Church affiliations

➤ Occupations

➤ Residences

➤ Anything else that can help identify the people listed on the sheet.

Name:	William Lynch[1,2]	
Birth:	abt 1797	County Meath in Ireland[3,1,4,5]
Death:	18 Nov 1849	Schuyler Falls, NY[1,4,6]
Occupation:	Stonemason. "He was an unexcelled mechanic (a mason by trade) and most worthy and respected citizen. He leaves a wife and 11 children."[6]	
Occupation:	Probably railroad laborer captured on 1850 census in Burke. At the same time, his wife was alone in Schuyler Falls with kids.[7]	
Father:	James Lynch (~1759-1838)	
Mother:	Catherine "Kitty" Watters (1771-)	
Marriage:	abt 1830	Ireland[8]

Spouse:	Ann "Catherine" Curran[9,10,11]	
Birth:	1810	Ireland[12,4,10,13]
Death:	27 Oct 1877[4,10]	

Children

1 M:	Patrick Curran "P.C." Lynch[14,15,1]	
Birth:	1832	County Meath in Ireland, a village about 20 miles from Tara Hall[1,14,16,17]
Death:	8 Jul 1919	Ogdensburg[18]
Spouse:	Mary Cowan	
Marriage:	2 Nov 1858	Married at St. Josephs Church by Father Thaye (?)[18]

2 M:	Michael Lynch[1,8]	
Birth:	24 Nov 1839	New York state[12,10,8]

You may need to incorporate a reference system for family group sheets, especially as you track the marriages for the children on each sheet. These families will then get their own group sheets. You will want to be able to quickly reference back and forth between the generations.

Some researchers like a simple numbering system similar to that used for pedigree charts. Others like to include last names with page numbers. There's no official system—just find a style that works for you.

Also keep in mind that if you use online or desktop genealogy software, your computer will do the hard work of creating references and linking families for you.

Research log

Genealogists are detectives. Working out puzzles is the name of our game! More than once I have sat at my computer until the wee hours of the morning because I got a break on a difficult line and ended up chasing rabbits all night. Once you get the genealogy bug, it is bound to happen to you, too!

But late-night research sessions can leave you with a headache the next morning, or a few weeks later, when you come back to review what you discovered. Where did you find that interesting clue about Uncle Chuck? What was the website that contained a list of 19th-Century burials in western Pennsylvania?

Smart genealogists log these details. They list websites that were visited, and note what was found at each one (if anything). If you were hot on the trail of an elusive ancestor, though, you may not have taken the time to keep a research log. This can cause problems later, when you can't remember where a certain piece of information came from, or you realize that you're looking at the same website for the twentieth time—and you still can't find what you're looking for!

Research logs do not have to be fancy. A paper notebook, a spreadsheet, or a text document on your computer work just fine. Whatever format you use, try to record the following types of information:

- ➤ Date(s) research was performed.
- ➤ Book, website consulted (including URL), person interviewed, etc.
  - ▷ Books: Record page numbers.
  - ▷ Websites: Note pages viewed, or location of specific resources (for instance, Home > Indexes > Marriage certificates > 1880s).
- ➤ Reference numbers for charts.
- ➤ What you found, or did not find, from each source.

Spreadsheets are covered in more detail in Chapter 5.

Other types of charts and forms

Pedigree charts, family group sheets, and research logs are not the only forms available to genealogists. There are established formats (described below) as well as custom versions that you can create on the fly to track various types of data.

My advice to anyone getting started is this: Create forms for your research as the need arises. For instance, if you find you need to have a sortable chart that lists dates of birth and places of birth for members of a certain branch of your family, then open up Microsoft Excel or Google Sheets and enter the data. Spreadsheets can be your friend!

Here are some examples:

- ➤ **Correspondence log.** Track who you contact and the information sought.

- ➤ **Useful websites.** Bookmark websites you frequently visit, then create a resource list showing what they contain and why it is useful to your research.

- ➤ **Genealogy road trip plans.** List libraries, archives, courthouses, or other facilities containing important records, listing their addresses, hours of operation, and other pertinent information.

- ➤ **Surname list/location list.** Compile a list of family surnames and the locations associated with each one, which can be helpful when traveling or conducting quick online searches.

- ➤ **Abbreviations and other terms.** Record government abbreviations, religious terms, and foreign words you come across in the course of your research.

Why source citations are so important

When you are recording names, dates, events, or some other piece of information, it is critical to take note of the source. A good family historian can always explain where a particular piece of research was found.

Showing proof gives credibility to your tree and saves work for future generations. Failing to take note of the source may indicate to others (or yourself, if you take another look) that the information is unconfirmed, hearsay, or otherwise unreliable—and therefore needs to be checked again. It also calls into question any research that is based on that piece of information.

What makes a good source citation? Consider this source citation for a 19th-Century Virginian, Caleb Cleveland:

> *Online chancery record for Caleb Cleveland.*

If someone else were to look at this citation, it would be clear that it was a reference to Caleb Cleveland, and it was sourced online. But so much other information is missing. What was the date of the original record, and what is its formal title? Where is it located online? What is the corresponding location of the record in the real world? Is there any other information that you or another researcher might find useful if referencing the citation later?

Here is the same record, properly cited:

> *Fairfax County, Virginia, Chancery Court File 1885-004 CFF#17p, Caleb Cleveland Jr. vs Beverly Lacy, 18 March 1884, pages 11-15 division of land with platt, digital images (http://www.lva.virginia.gov : accessed 18 August 2015); Library of Virginia, Richmond.*

The format may look familiar. Think back to when you were in school. Do you remember writing research reports, and creating a bibliography or footnotes to document your sources? One of my high school English teachers took citations very seriously, noting that not all sources are equal. She taught us to analyze how good the source was. We also had to determine if multiple sources all referenced the same original document or book. The teacher then encouraged us to go find the original source of the information. By getting to the original source, our research would be much stronger and informed.

This does not mean you need to write a research paper for every person in your family. Rather, I want to drive home the fact that knowing the sources of each piece of information can be crucial to understanding your family's stories.

Good source citations can also help other family members in the future. At some point, you may be contacted by a distant cousin who is researching the same line. When sharing information, it looks a heck of a lot better if your sources are properly documented. It also saves time—they will not need to track down and re-document everything you sent them. You may save yourself a lot of time if you need to go back to a piece of information 20 or 30 years later!

How to create good source citations

Evidence Explained: Citing History Sources from Artifacts to Cyberspace by Elizabeth Shown Mills is an excellent guide for creating genealogy source citations from scratch. It is called "The Bible" by many in the field, and is considered the go-to resource for anyone conducting serious family research. You can purchase the hardcover book online or download it to your tablet, computer, or phone from her *www.evidenceexplained.com*.

If a formal system for creating source citations sounds too daunting, don't worry. Just make sure you collect and write down as much information from the record as possible while you are looking at it. Your goal is to gather all of the important details and help lead future researchers (maybe even yourself) back to this document many years later. If you are using genealogy software, you will be able to generate easy-to-understand references or footnotes when outputting reports or other documents.

16. "1875 New York State Census for Newfane, Niagara County," Newfane, Niagara County, June 3-4, 1875, Photocopy of transcription, Niagara County Historian's Office, Lockport, New York, Spelled "Ellen:".
17. Cemetery records, St. Patrick's, Lockport, St. Patrick's, Lockport, NY, Copy of register, Niagara County Historian's office, Spelled "Helen" in two locations in cemetery records.
18. "1865 New York, State Census, District 02, Lockport, Niagara, New York, United States ," District 02, Lockport, Niagara, New York, United States, 1865
19. "New York, State Census, 1855, Royalton, Niagara, New York," Royalton, Niagara, New York, United States, 1855, Photo, FamilySearch (https://familysearch.org/pal:/MM9.1.1/K67Y-7XX : accessed 18 January 2015)
20. "1870 United States Census, Newfane, NY," New York Niagara Newfane, 1870, Photo, Household ID: 618 , Line Number: 9
21. Cemetery records, St. Patrick's, Lockport, St. Patrick's, Lockport, NY, Copy of register, Niagara County Historian's office.
22. "Interview with Marjorie Lamont (Heary), and maybe Duane, made on Buffalo hospital pamphlet," about 1975,

Here is a short list of information you might jot down if you encounter an interesting record:

➤ Title

➤ Author(s) (if given)

➤ Who published/created/edited the work

➤ Dates of publication or creation

➤ Certificate numbers (for vital records)

➤ Page numbers

➤ Column numbers for newspaper articles

➤ Website URLs with the date you first accessed the information

➤ Institution, place, or person who holds the source document

Write this data on the back of the copied document and in a source file on your computer so you have a record of it all. I know it seems redundant to put it in two places, but trust me, it will be helpful later on if you lose a piece of paper or your hard drive crashes. Be prepared!

PITFALL: Government records are not perfect

Government forms are filled out by officials, clerks, and other employees. Like all people, government workers sometimes make mistakes. There is also the possibility of the wrong information being given to clerks, either by accident or on purpose. In addition, the more people who participate in the creation of a record or document, the higher the chance for errors to be introduced. This is why genealogists carefully evaluate the documents they unearth, even vital records. It is not uncommon to discover that information on a person's birth and death certificates do not match. If you discover such a discrepancy, don't panic. Make a note of the conflicting data, and do a little digging to determine which source is correct.

Save time with templates

If you are comfortable creating templates in Microsoft Word, Google Docs, or some other word-processing program, consider creating templates to streamline the repetitive tasks associated with your research. Besides fillable forms, there may be opportunities to produce templates for other types of information. Once you get into your research groove, look at what you have collected and think of what types of templates would make your life easier.

Consider source citations. American genealogists often turn to the U.S. Census for their research. Instead of creating a source citation on the fly, create a template that you can pull out whenever you need to cite a new census record. It could look like this:

> [Year] U.S. Census, [county] , [state] , [type of schedule] , [district / township / ward] , p. [page number] , dwelling [number] , family [number] , [person or family of interest] ; digital image, [website title] ([URL], accessed [date]) ; [credit information] .

What does the resulting record look like? Here's an example based on the census template:

> 1880 U.S. Census, New York, New York population schedule, New York City, page 178 (stamped), dwelling 51, family 353, Jahnke family; digital image (*http://www.ancestry.com*, accessed 2013); citing Family History Film: *1254893*.

Templates can come in handy in other situations, too. If you find that you are constantly reaching out to relatives and repositories, consider creating a template for your correspondence. It should have all the general information required, so you just need to update the specifics of your query each time you send out a letter.

Templates can also be used for the following types of information:

➤ Gravestone inscriptions

➤ Abstracts of other people's research

➤ Interview transcripts

Write it all down: Journaling your way to success

Did you keep a diary as a child? Perhaps you maintained a more detailed journal when you took an extended cross-country trip or were stationed overseas. In genealogy, we encourage people to keep logs, journals, and notebooks (either on paper or digital) to keep track of all aspects of their research. Your first genealogy journal, however, should be about *you*. Remember, it all starts at home!

It does not have to be a bound journal. Heck, get out a piece of scrap paper or sit down with your tablet or laptop and simply start writing... about you! It could become the first document about you for your research files, an ongoing memoir for future generations. You do not need a computer or any fancy forms to get started. Just talk about your family and put to paper everything you know and remember. For me, this type of journal quickly became a place to gather my thoughts and research ideas, and chronicle what I was doing or memories I had.

Information to include in your genealogy journal

Start simple, with your name and any other information that can explain or identify you. From there you can branch out into as much detail as you want. For example, you might want to cover the following pieces of information:

➤ The date (always document when you create something)

➤ Your name and nicknames

➤ Date and place of birth

➤ Your parents and grandparents and their dates and places of birth

➤ Spouse and marriage details

➤ Information about children

➤ Schools attended and degrees/certifications obtained

➤ Dates associated with a baptism, First Communion, Bar Mitzvah, etc.

➤ Military service details, such as deployments, commendations, etc.

Why should you take the trouble to write down all of this information? Simply put, you are the best person to record your personal history. Take the time to write it now, and continue to add to it. The journal will be a treasure to those who come after you. What you add to these pages, and how much detail, is completely up to you. However, it will provide the clues that future generations use to research you and in turn uncover the documents that go with your life.

Don't feel obliged to write an autobiography, though. After you get to a good point with your story, turn to other family members. Do a page for each of your parents, your spouse, children, siblings, grandparents, aunts, uncles, and cousins. Write down what you know about each of them. You can write down basic facts or add longer stories. These pages contain the clues to the documents you want to gather for your research. Those documents are the facts, and these stories breathe life into them.

Writing about other family members

I grew up with stories about my grandfather, a former Golden Gloves boxer. He died when I was just 2, and I have only one really clear memory about him. Everything else I know about him was told to me by my family.

For instance, my grandmother loved relating the story of how he was cheated out of getting a place on the 1936 U.S. Olympic Team! The story involved a questionable ruling during a qualifying fight in Chicago. She would get so worked up about the crowd booing the judges. Until the day he died, people from our small town would tell him he would have been a great Olympic contender!

It's a great story. But it was even better when I found the newspaper articles about the fight. The crowd did indeed boo the results! The story was real and I made sure to write about it in my journal.

PROTIP: Memories for the next generation

The holy grail for most family genealogists is a diary written by an ancestor, or a family Bible with notes about family members in the endpapers. They are amazing finds that give you wonderful insights about family makeup, interactions, and the social history of your ancestors.

Just as an old journal can be a treasure for current generations, it's good practice to think of how you can prepare similar documents for future generations. A few years ago, I bought journals for my parents and my husband's parents. In them I placed 20 questions that their grandchildren wanted to have answered about their lives. Then I encouraged them to continue writing about their pasts, their families, memories, funny anecdotes, sad events . . . really, anything they wanted their children and grandchildren to know about them. These journals will not only be wonderful genealogical documents but also wonderful family heirlooms. In the Appendix, there is a list of 20 questions to ask your own relatives!

Case Study: Rose's quest to discover her African-American ancestors

Rose is keen to explore her African-American heritage. It is important to her to honor the memories of her slave ancestors. However, finding them may be an uphill battle.

Numerous brick walls are associated with researching slave families. When the slave ships that had completed the Middle Passage were unloaded at ports on the East and Gulf coasts, slaves' names were seldom recorded. Moreover, until Emancipation in 1865, families were frequently broken up. Of the limited records that were kept, many were destroyed during the Civil War or in disasters such as floods.

Rose decided to turn to her extended family. She interviewed older family members and asked each of them to write down family memories. Rose hopes to find clues to her history in their stories and has determined some common threads. Rose has begun the serious research. She started to look at deeds, tax records, and online resources. The work can be tedious at times, but it is important to her and her family. Some day, she knows she will walk upon the same ground her ancestors once tread, and she will be able to properly pay her respects.

CHAPTER 5

Preserving records and research

One person's mess is merely another person's filing system.
—*Margo Kaufman*

It should come as no surprise that most "genies" don't care for the various tasks associated with preserving the fruits of their research. Who likes to file paperwork? The thrill of the chase—tracking down ancestors and solving family mysteries—is where all of the fun takes place!

Yet filing cannot be ignored for long. Keeping up with filing and long-term storage is something that I have to force myself to do, or I risk ending up with piles of documents around my office and oddly labeled folders on my computer. Don't let this happen to you!

Generally speaking, there are three types of items genealogists need to organize:

➤ Paper items

➤ Digital items

➤ Heirlooms and ephemera

The last category can include anything from your grandmother's Bakelite jewelry to a family Bible from the 1850s.

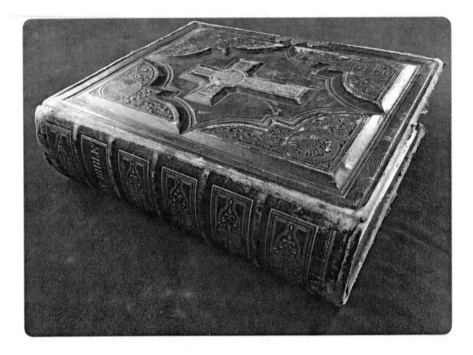

By the end of this chapter, I want you to identify a method of organizing and filing records that works for you . . . and stick with it! It's fine to cobble together several different techniques. The important thing is, as long as the method makes sense to you, and is relatively easy to follow, use it. Switching to a new-fangled system every few years can lead to disaster. It's possible to lose papers, forget where you stored important items, or derail promising lines of inquiry.

How to tame sprawling records

Genealogy takes up space. It may start with a single folder or a desk drawer, but over time the collection of papers, photos, research tools, and other items will grow to take up more and more space. At times, it may seem that the piles of papers, photos, and other records are multiplying when your back is turned!

That is what happened with me. Once the genealogy bug bit, I could not stop. I gathered, printed, and saved copies of everything I found. Soon my entire kitchen table, and most of the floor around it, was covered with piles of books and documents. After nearly 3 months, my family asked me if the table was ever going to be used for eating again. Eventually I gave into their demands. (Plus, my husband bought me a desk.)

While you may want to stay small, you should still plan for the future when new records or donations from family members start to pile up on your desk. Think about how you could accommodate a growing collection. For instance, you you could take one of the following steps:

➤ Standardize your storage by using one type of binder, folder, or storage box that you can easily buy as your storage needs grow.

➤ Find room to add a bookshelf or filing cabinet in an area of the house dedicated to your research.

➤ When purchasing a desk, consider buying one that can hold hanging files.

➤ Find an out-of-the-way and safe place to store important items.

PROTIP: Everyone loves a sale!

A good time to buy supplies for organizing and storing genealogy records is right after school starts, when retailers are trying to clear the shelves of back-to-school supplies. You will find great deals on binders, folders, and whatever else you need for your research.

A question of organization

So you have found a place to store all of your genealogy records. But how do you organize them?

Color-coding and numbering systems are two of the more common methods to organize genealogy files. If you are a visual person, it might make sense to associate different families with differently colored labels. Others may prefer an alphanumeric system that follows a logical order.

Organizing records using colors

If you like the idea of color-coding records, there are several different ways you can do it:

> **By surname.** This method uses a large variety of colors, as each surname in your family tree will have a different color. Some genealogists use folders or binders with different colored dots to show which lines married into others.

> **By paternal or maternal lines.** Most people choose to use a two-color method, one for the father's family and one for the mother's family. However, it is also possible to use a four-color system in which each grandparent's line has its own color.

> **By type of record.** Some people like to file their papers for each surname by record type. Birth records end up in a red binder, while marriage records go into the white binder, and death records are filed in a black binder.

Color-coding can be used for paper records or digital records. For paper records, you can use colored markers, stickers, or labels. For digital records, determine if your computer or software program supports applying colored labels to individual files or folders.

Organizing records using a numbering system

Numbering systems may appear complex. However, there are several standard systems that are not only logical, but also are easy to apply. In fact, many genealogy software programs can automatically apply the systems to your tree.

Here is a short list of common systems:

➤ **Ancestor numbering systems.** The most well-known example is the Ahnentafel (German for "ancestor table") system for direct-line ancestors. It is similar to the scheme used in Pedigree Charts, covered in Chapter 4, and logically assigns a number value to each ancestor based on his or her gender, generation, and branch. An example is shown below.

➤ **Descendant numbering systems.** These work on the descendants of a particular ancestor. The Modified Register System is one example.

➤ **Home-grown numbering systems.** Some family genealogists create their own numbering systems. It is usually an alphanumeric system which they can use in reports, files, databases, and anywhere else to reference a specific person in their tree. For example, I could label any document associated with myself "CB-1" which includes the initials of my last names (Combs-Bennett) and the number 1 because I am the first person in the tree with that surname. Different codes could be used for other people in the tree.

Ancestors of James Robert Alexander

Generation 1

1. **James Robert Alexander**, son of Joseph Alexander and Abigail McKnitt, was born in 1690 in Manokin (Somerset County), Somerset County, Maryland, USA. He died on 31 May 1779 in Cecil, MD. He married **Margaret Abigail McKnitt** in 1713 in Cecil, MD. She was born on 26 Dec 1693 in Manokin, Somerset, MD. She died on 31 Jul 1736 in Cecil County, Maryland, USA. He married **Margaret McKnitt**. She was born in 1714.

Generation 2

2. **Joseph Alexander**, son of William Alexander and Mary Maxwell, was born in 1660 in Raphoe, County Donegal, Ireland. He died on 09 Mar 1730 in Cecil County, Maryland, USA. He married **Abigail McKnitt** in 1686 in MD.

3. **Abigail McKnitt**, daughter of John McKnitt-McKnight and Elizabeth Wallace, was born in 1667 in Manokin (Somerset County), Somerset County, Maryland, USA. She died on 23 Dec 1714 in Cecil County, Maryland, USA.

    Abigail McKnitt and Joseph Alexander had the following child:

    1.   i.   James Robert Alexander was born in 1690 in Manokin (Somerset County), Somerset County, Maryland, USA. He died on 31 May 1779 in Cecil, MD. He married Margaret Abigail McKnitt in 1713 in Cecil, MD. She was born on 26 Dec 1693 in Manokin, Somerset, MD. She died on 31 Jul 1736 in Cecil County, Maryland, USA. He married Margaret McKnitt. She was born in 1714.

Generation 3

4. **William Alexander** was born in 1625 in Scotland. He died in 1688 in Manokin (Somerset County), Somerset County, Maryland, USA. He married **Mary Maxwell**.

5. **Mary Maxwell** was born in 1625 in UI.

    Mary Maxwell and William Alexander had the following children:

    i.   William Alexander was born in 1646

Naming conventions for paper files and digital records

Creating a consistent naming system across your digital and paper files will make your life much easier. Use the same naming standards across all media. Changing the way you abbreviate, or the order in which you write something, will make it harder for you to find what you are looking for years later when you unearth a new clue for a particular relative.

One approach for records is to create a set of standard file abbreviations for different record sets. For example, you could use the following codes on your files:

➤ BC = birth certificate

➤ DC = death certificate

➤ MC = marriage certificate

➤ WILL = will or probate record

➤ LND = land record or deed

When you combine a record abbreviation with a surname and date, you have a very nice way to quickly determine what you are looking at.

Such a system can easily be extended to digital records. For example, let's say I download a death certificate for Mary Smith from 1907. I would label the image "Smith_Mary_DC_1907" and save it to the Smith folder on my hard drive.

For certain records, you might find yourself with a digital image and a paper copy. By using the same naming system, you can tie the records together and then create an index to place in a binder or file folder for easier reference later on.

File Name	Record Name	Digital File Name	Page
Smith Family	Smith, Edward BC 1860	Smith_Edward_BC_1860	1
	Jones and Smith MC 1880	Jones_Smith_MC_1880	2
	Smith, Mary DC 1907	Smith_Mary_DC_1907	3

> ### PROTIP: Merging and purging files
>
> From time to time, you may need to merge or purge files. A typical scenario involves finding duplicate items—for instance, you may find a copy of an old family letter, and then your aunt sends you a copy of the same document. When this happens you should stop and think about the following:
>
> ➤ Are they unique or identical?
>
> ➤ Is one a better copy?
>
> ➤ Should they be merged into one file or the duplicates purged?
>
> Regularly merging and purging records will help your research (and your sanity!) in the long run.

Using spreadsheets to record inventory and other data

Spreadsheet software is a genealogist's best friend. We use spreadsheets not only to help with analysis but also to keep track of documents, photographs, and other pieces of family history. If you are not already comfortable with spreadsheet software on your computer, you should take some time to learn more about it. It will make your life as a family history researcher much, much easier!

When relatives identify you as the family historian, all kinds of stuff will begin to appear on your doorstep—some wonderful, some broken, and some of questionable origin. Spreadsheets are a great way to keep track of items and their provenance for future generations.

Spreadsheets can be used to track the following items:

➤ Documents by type, date, or surname

➤ Photos

➤ Digital records

➤ Books relevant to your research

➤ Lectures

➤ Websites and other online repositories

➤ Lists of people

Microsoft Excel and Google Sheets are two popular spreadsheet applications. Both have similar functionality. Excel is more powerful, but Google Sheets is free and is optimized for online and mobile use, as shown below.

First & Mid Na	Last Name	Birth - Death	Birth Place	# of Children
Julia	Bracken	1849-1898		2
Robert	Brado			1
Robert	Brado			0
	Brady	~-1919		6
Hugh	Brady			1
Albert V.	Brennan	~1891->1926	United States	0
Andrew	Brennan	~1855->1922	United States	7
Andrew	Brennan	~1856-	New York state	0
Ann	Brennan	~1868-	Newfane	0
Catherine	Brennan	~1863-	New York state	0

PROTIP: Learning how to use spreadsheets

Spreadsheets may seem daunting at first, but they are powerful tools for managing data. Check out *Excel Basics In 30 Minutes* to learn how to use Excel or Google Sheets. Once you start, you will find yourself making spreadsheets for all kinds of data.

Using hardware and other equipment to organize and store records

We may be living in a digital age, but genealogists still collect a lot of paper. Technology can help reduce the need for paper, though. To help tame the clutter, a good portable scanner or digital camera is key (we talked about such items being a part of your research kit back in Chapter 2.) You can easily scan papers and documents while on research trips, visiting family members, or at libraries. If you do not own a scanner, take a picture with your digital camera or smartphone. Voila, one less piece of paper for you to store or misplace!

A good label maker for your growing collection of stuff can also help. Many people print off labels from their computer for larger items, but a small handheld one is ideal for the small items you come into contact with. In addition to a label maker, a paper shredder should be considered. (It may seem an odd addition but we can't keep everything, and we do not want someone finding a copy of a vital record in the trash.)

Computer file formats, from GEDCOM to PNG

Genealogists employ a number of software tools to keep ancestors and charts in order. There are three general approaches:

1. **DIY.** Use word processors, drawing programs, and other standard desktop productivity software to create family trees, group sheets, and other records.

2. **Desktop genealogy software.** Genealogy applications for Windows, Mac, and Linux PCs let users store records and create trees and charts. An example is shown below.

3. **Online software.** Several genealogy websites and online databases let registered users create and share virtual trees, save historical records, and organize family files.

There are pros and cons to each approach, as well as different pricing options. While it is possible to use Microsoft Word and graphics programs to create records and draw family trees, prepackaged desktop software or online tools can save lots of time and make it easy to organize information and find specific records.

Take some time to research what's available. Several companies offer free trial periods, which are useful for checking out the features of the software.

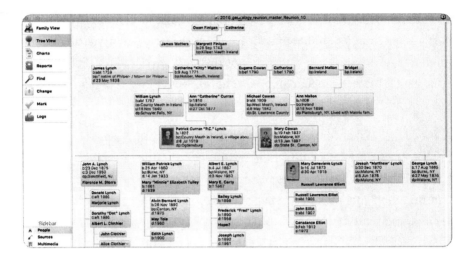

When it comes to saving digital files, an important consideration is creating files that can be transferred to other applications—and can still be opened 20 years later! Many people who bought early desktop genealogy programs in the 1980s and 1990s are now unable to open obsolete file formats. You may also discover that a popular online family tree program is incompatible with the tools used by relatives with whom you want to share information.

While it is impossible to know what the future holds when it comes to storing genealogy data, a good rule of thumb is to use established standards for storing copies of your data. In the genealogy world, file formats include:

> **Text is a reliable file format for long-term storage.** Most computers can save and read text files, and will likely be able to read the same files decades later. However, text documents do not preserve formatting.

> **CSV is a text-based format for storing spreadsheet files as comma-separated values.** Excel and other spreadsheet programs can import and export .csv files.

> **Portable Network Graphics (PNG) files are a standard way to store digital images, based on an international open standard.** Unlike JPEG images, PNG files are lossless, meaning images will not be downgraded through compression or other space-saving algorithms.

➤ **GEDCOM is an older text-based format for storing genealogy data (see sample below).** Many desktop and online genealogy programs let users upload and download GEDCOM files.

```
2 SOUR @S177@
1 OCCU Gardener
2 SOUR @S46@
2 SOUR @S177@
1 HOMEADDRESS 27 Bowery, Newport, Rhode Island (1889)
1 OCCU Quarterman, U.S. Government (Obituary says "outside quaterman, Torpedo
Station". He started working there in 1901
2 SOUR @S58@
2 SOUR @S60@
1 HOBB Father Mathew Total Abstinence Society. Member since aged 14, president
1894-1917.
2 SOUR @S60@
1 HOBB Recreation Commission, liked to officiate at athletic events
2 SOUR @S60@
1 OBJE
2 FORM jpg
2 FILE ~/Documents/home/GENEALOGY/Newport Genealogy/Newport Historical Society
081611/DSCN1066.JPG
2 TITL DSCN1066
2 _TYPE PHOTO
2 _PRIM Y
2 _SIZE 4000.000000 3000.000000
1 FAMC @F243@
1 CHAN
2 DATE 17 JAN 2015
0 @I323@ INDI
1 _UID FAE4C58D430E42D6891A7E2667F728147A58
1 NAME Mary E. A. /Doherty/
2 SOUR @S41@
```

PITFALL: Obsolete file formats

A file format that is controlled by a single company or organization—think Microsoft Word documents (.docx) or Adobe PDF files—may not survive if the company fails or decides to discontinue the product line. This is exactly what happened with obsolete formats associated with long-gone programs such as WordPerfect, Lotus 1-2-3, and Personal Ancestral File (PAF). It may be possible to find software programs that can still open discontinued formats, but over time, such options will disappear.

Planning for disasters

Imagine how you would feel if you suddenly lost access to all of your genealogy records. Computer failures, fires, flooding, or some other disaster could wipe out years of research in an instant. For this reason, it is critical to make backups of your data, including family trees, documents, photos, spreadsheets, logs, and anything else related to your research.

Making digital copies of paper documents is one way to protect your research. But it doesn't stop there—backing up digital files is also crucial.

While it is possible to copy files onto external drives, the digital backups may also become corrupted or damaged. Therefore, you may want to invest in an automatic backup service that will regularly create remote backups of the files on your computer. Popular services include:

➤ Carbonite (*carbonite.com*)

➤ Dropbox (*dropbox.com*)

➤ Google Drive (*drive.google.com*)

➤ Microsoft OneDrive (*onedrive.live.com*)

The added advantage of many of these platforms is they allow you to share files with other people. For instance, let's say you want to share a collection of photographs of your Great-Grandfather Emmet C. Lancaster with your cousins. Using these services, it is possible to share a link to the folder containing the photos so they can easily take a look, download copies to their own computers, or even contribute photos from their collections.

PROTIP: Learning how to use online storage services

Dropbox and Google Drive are two popular online storage services that allow users to easily store documents, photos, and other files. Both services provide mobile apps to view documents on your phone or tablet. For more information on how to get started with these two services, check out *Dropbox In 30 Minutes* and *Google Drive & Docs In 30 Minutes*.

Case study: Margaret's new approach to organizing records and heirlooms

Margaret did not excel at keeping things organized. Rather, she tended to build up piles of stuff everywhere in her house.

Margaret's mindset changed after her mother died. As she was cleaning the house, she discovered so many amazing things in her mother's attic. She vowed to better sort, organize, and store everything she brought home.

She enlisted some friends to help. Together, they cleared her guest room and transformed it into a well-organized storage space using plastic organizers, shelving units, and a filing cabinet she bought on sale. After that, it was a matter of taking the time to put letters, photos, family records, heirlooms and other items in order, using color-coded folders and binders for various branches of the family.

Margaret also created digital copies of everything she found in her mother's house and backed them up using an online storage service. She lives in an area that is prone to tornadoes, and she does not want to lose everything to a storm. With backups, something will survive if her house gets hit.

Long-term, Margaret hopes to connect with cousins who may know more about the people shown in the old photos or mentioned in the faded letters. She is building an online family tree that other family members can see and add to.

Conclusion

Over the past 30 minutes, you have received an introduction to genealogy that can help you trace your family history. While there is still a lot to learn, you should feel confident about grasping the basic principles and avoiding some common pitfalls.

Now it is time to put what you have learned to the test! Gather your records and print out some blank forms. Buy a few binders and storage totes, and clear off a shelf in your closet to store them. Get your portable genealogy research kit ready, and make plans for a genealogy road trip to your grand-mother's hometown to visit the municipal records office and the local cemetery. You are in for an amazing journey into your family's past!

It need not be a lonely quest. Regard it as an opportunity to connect with relatives to share discoveries and stories. You can also take the quest online, to conduct research, build an online tree, and discuss family surnames with other researchers.

There are many additional resources to turn to. The companion website to this book has blog posts, blank genealogy forms, and other information. It is located at *genealogy.in30minutes.com*. Local bookstores and libraries may have books and genealogy magazines to aid your research. Keep informed about the world of genealogy and take the time to branch out.

If you are interested in learning about more advanced topics, I encourage you to watch webinars, take online courses, or attend lectures in your local area. Family Search has a large number of online videos and free lessons available at *familysearch.org*. Fee-based courses can be found at Family Tree

University (*familytreeuniversity.com*) and The National Institute for Genealogical Studies (*genealogicalstudies.com*).

It has been my pleasure guiding you through the basics of genealogy research. Making the effort to understand your family's origins is a rewarding pursuit, and I hope this book can help you get started on the right foot. If you want to learn more about who I am, please visit my blog at *tntfamilyhistory.blogspot.com* or follow my latest adventures on twitter via @tntfamhist.

Finally, if you have a few minutes to spare, I would greatly appreciate it if you could leave a review of this book online. Honest reviews let other people know what to expect, and greatly raise the profile of *Genealogy Basics In 30 Minutes*. My book is going up against competing titles from large publishing houses, so every review counts.

Thanks for reading!

Shannon Combs-Bennett

About the Author

Shannon Combs-Bennett is an author, researcher, and lecturer based in the Washington, D.C. metro area. She regularly speaks and writes about genetic genealogy, Virginia genealogy, and research methods. Shannon is a frequent contributor to *Family Tree Magazine* and Family Tree University, serves as the Creative Director for The In-Depth Genealogist, and owns T2 Family History. She earned her Bachelor of Science in Biology from Indiana University, which started her passion for research and genetic genealogy. Shannon completed the Boston University Certificate of Genealogical Research in 2013 and is a student at the National Institute for Genealogical Studies, earning a certificate in American Records. *Genealogy Basics In 30 Minutes* is her third book.

Appendix

Pedigree chart

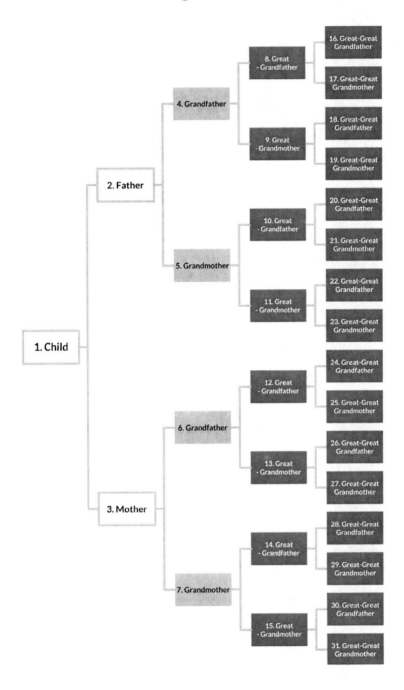

Cousin chart

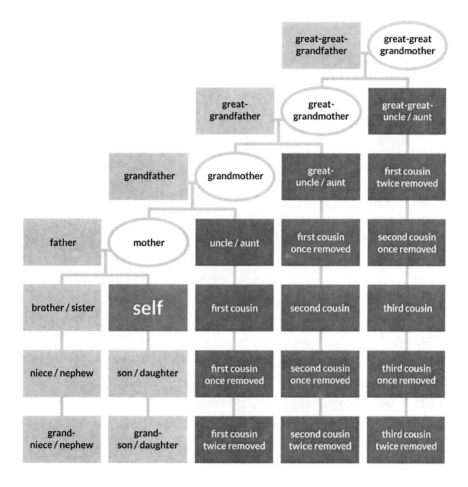

Getting kids involved:
20 questions to ask relatives

To help my parents pass on their memories to their grandchildren, we gave them journals. My kids wrote out 20 questions they wanted their grandparents to answer. What made them wonderful and unique is that they were full of childhood wonder about who these adults were. Asking simple questions can open the door to more memories. I encouraged my parents to elaborate as they saw fit. In some instances, the answers were pages long. We now have wonderful family heirlooms for future generations. These journals will give readers insights into personalities in ways that vital records cannot.

Here are the questions:

1. What is your favorite color?
2. What is your earliest memory?
3. When did you learn to drive?
4. What was your first car?
5. Which historical events that you lived through are the most memorable to you?
6. Do you have a favorite flavor of ice cream?
7. Who were your grandparents?
8. Did you play sports?
9. What did you do during summer vacation from school?
10. Where did you go to school?
11. Did you have any pets?
12. Where were you born?
13. Did you join clubs as a kid?
14. What was your first job?
15. Tell me about your wedding.
16. Tell me about your brothers and sisters.
17. Tell me what my mom (or dad) was like as a kid.
18. Can you ride a bike?
19. Who was your favorite teacher in school?
20. Did you go to any high school dances?

Index

Notes

CPSIA information can be obtained
at www.ICGtesting.com
Printed in the USA
FFOW02n1120020217
31943FF